MW01045557

# Influences
## on Sexuality

## Understanding Their Effects

### By Judith Peacock

Consultant:
Jennifer A. Oliphant, MPH
Research Fellow and Community Outreach Coordinator
National Teen Pregnancy Prevention Research Center
Division of General Pediatrics and Adolescent Health
University of Minnesota

Perspectives on Healthy Sexuality

**LifeMatters**
an imprint of Capstone Press
Mankato, Minnesota

**LifeMatters** books are published by Capstone Press
PO Box 669 • 151 Good Counsel Drive • Mankato, Minnesota 56002
*http://www.capstone-press.com*

Printed in the United States of America

## Library of Congress Cataloging-in-Publication Data
Peacock, Judith, 1942–
    Influences on sexuality: understanding their effects / by Judith Peacock.
         p.      cm.—(Perspectives on healthy sexuality)
    Includes bibliographical references and index.
    ISBN 0-7368-0714-4 (hard cover) ISBN 0-7368-8843-8 (soft cover)
    1.Teenagers—Sexual behavior—Juvenile literature. 2. Sex—Juvenile literature.
    [1. Youth—Sexual behavior. 2. Sexual ethics.] I. Title. II. Series.
    HQ27 .P4 2001
    306.7′0835—dc21                       00-031336
                                          CIP

Summary: Discusses the different aspects of sexuality and the influences that shape sexuality, such as family, peers, school, media and popular culture, religion, and law.

## Staff Credits
Rebecca Aldridge, editor; Adam Lazar, designer; Kim Danger, photo researcher
Production by Stacey Field

## Photo Credits
Cover: ©PhotoDisc/Barbara Penoyar
©Artvillc, 47
©DigitalVision, 26
International Stock/©Andre Jenny, 52
Photo Network/©Esbin-Anderson, 8; ©Myrleen Cate, 13; ©Stephen Agricola, 37
©Stockbyte, 20, 31
Unicorn Stock Photos/©Jeff Greenberg, 10; ©Novastock, 34; ©A. Ramey, 50
Uniphoto/38, ©Llewellyn, 19, 24; ©J. Smith, 43; ©Frank Siteman, 57
Visuals Unlimited/©Robert Clay, 29; ©Jeff Greenberg, 45

A 0 9 8 7 6 5 4 3 2 1

# Table of Contents

## Chapter Overview

A person's sexuality affects every aspect of his or her life. It affects a person's body, mind, emotions, and relationships.

Sexuality is complicated because it has many parts. While sexuality includes sexual intercourse, it includes body image and sensuality as well. Gender identity, gender role, sexual orientation, and sexual attitudes, behaviors, and likes and dislikes are part of sexuality, too.

Both biological and social factors shape a person's sexuality. These influences can be positive or negative.

# Chapter 1

## What Is Sexuality?

The word *sexuality* contains that little word *sex*. Sexuality, however, is much more than sexual intercourse. Sexuality involves your body, mind, emotions, and relationships. It forms an important part of your personality and affects all areas of your life.

### More Than Sex Organs

Sexuality can be complicated because it has many parts. It includes sensuality, body image, gender identity and role, sexual orientation, and sexual attitudes, behaviors, and likes and dislikes.

### Sensuality

Sensuality refers to the senses. Touching, seeing, hearing, tasting, and smelling are all part of sexuality. Certain sensory experiences can bring about sexual feelings and desires. For example, the smell of aftershave or perfume might turn a person on. Couples might play romantic music to set the mood for making love. Touch is perhaps the most sexually stimulating of the senses. Caressing, hugging, and kissing can feel wonderful.

## Body Image

Body image is a person's mental picture of how he or she looks. It includes how the person feels about his or her body. A person's inner picture may or may not reflect how others see him or her. Many people are unhappy with their body image. People with a negative body image may feel that no one could be attracted to them. They may shut themselves off from dating and having other close relationships.

Junior is a high school senior. He is cute, **Junior, Age 18** smart, and talented. Still, he doesn't feel too good about himself. The reason is his size. Junior always has been short for his age. All his life his friends and family have teased him about being so little. As a result, Junior doesn't feel he measures up to other guys. He's never been on a date because he thinks girls would be embarrassed to go out with a short, skinny guy like himself.

People who are transgender identify with the opposite gender. A male feels like a female while a female feels like a male. Transgenders feel like they are trapped in the wrong body. They may use hormone therapy and surgery to change their body so it matches their gender identity. If they do this, they are referred to as transsexual.

**Gender Identity**

The word *gender* refers to being male or female. Gender identity is a person's sense of being male or female, or having traits thought to be masculine or feminine. The person thinks "I am a male" or "I am a female."

Masculine and feminine traits can be inborn characteristics such as body shape and height. Broad shoulders, facial hair, a muscular build, and a deep voice often are considered masculine. A soft voice, soft skin, and a rounded, curvy body often are considered feminine. Masculine and feminine traits also can be characteristics that people acquire. Clothing and hairstyle, for instance, often set women apart from men.

Ideas about masculinity and femininity vary from culture to culture. Americans generally believe that males should be independent, aggressive, and competitive. They often believe that females should be tender, emotional, dependent, and noncompetitive. People who don't conform to the traits of their gender may be ridiculed or rejected. Fortunately, many people now recognize that males and females can share a lot of the same traits.

### Gender Role

Gender role refers to the behavior expected of a male or female. Until about 30 years ago, women in North America were expected to be homemakers. They stayed at home and took care of the house and children. Men were expected to be the breadwinners. They held a job and earned money to support the family. These traditional gender roles, especially for women, have changed a lot.

Gender identity and gender roles are closely related. They frequently reflect stereotypes. A stereotype is a general idea applied to all individuals in a group. For example, some people believe that females are too weak and emotional for jobs that require strength and endurance. Examples of such jobs include fire fighting and construction work. Likewise, some people believe that men cannot do jobs typically linked to women, such as being a nurse or secretary. These sex-role stereotypes can limit a person's opportunities.

**Personality traits**

Men: Self-confident, aggressive, decisive
Women: Willing to please, gentle, understanding

Physical appearance

Men: Tall, broad-shouldered, muscular
Women: Small, graceful

Gender roles affect sexual relationships as well. In North America, it's been customary for the male to take the lead. The man often has been the one expected to ask a woman out on a date or to propose marriage. Men have been expected to initiate sexual intercourse. In recent years, it's become more acceptable for a woman to start up a relationship with a man. Gender roles in sexual relationships can help people know how to act, but they also can create tension and worry.

Susie's in agony. She likes Tan, a boy in her biology class, and wants him to ask her to the school dance. She has tried everything to get Tan to ask her—smiling at him, flirting, dropping hints. Susie is sure Tan likes her, and she knows he hasn't asked anyone else. "What's with him, anyway?" she wonders.

**Susie, Age 15**

Susie is thinking about asking Tan to the dance. After all, lots of girls ask out boys these days. Then she thinks, "What if he turns me down? I'd have the double embarrassment of not being asked and of being rejected!"

Finally, Susie makes a decision. "I'm going to do it. I'm going to call him. Even if Tan turns me down, at least I'll finally know how he feels."

### Sexual Orientation

Sexual orientation means the gender to which a person is physically and emotionally attracted. People attracted to the opposite gender have heterosexual attractions. People attracted to their own gender have homosexual attractions. Males attracted to other males are called gay. Females attracted to other females are called lesbian. People attracted to both genders are bisexual.

No one knows for sure what determines sexual orientation. Strong evidence points to genetic factors that we're born with. Rather than being a conscious choice, sexual orientation may be programmed into a person's genes. A child's sexual orientation is set by puberty. This is the time when physical changes allow the body to reproduce, or create a baby.

About 10 percent of the population is homosexual. People who are gay or lesbian may have difficulty adjusting to their sexuality. They may face prejudice and harassment from individuals who fear or disapprove of homosexuality.

Stereotypes also exist for gays and lesbians. Some people think all lesbians have short hair, deep voices, and muscular bodies. This is a description of the so-called "butch" lesbian. Some people think all gay men have high voices and delicate looks. This describes the so-called "effeminate" gay. Like heterosexuals, lesbians and gays may or may not have these characteristics. Judging any people using stereotypes is always unfair.

**Sexual Attitudes, Behaviors, and Likes and Dislikes**

Sexuality includes a person's attitudes toward sexual behavior and sexual relationships. These attitudes may be healthy or unhealthy. People with a healthy attitude view sex as a pleasurable activity within a loving relationship. They protect themselves from the risks of intercourse such as unplanned pregnancy or sexually transmitted diseases (STDs). These diseases are spread during sexual contact with someone already infected. People with an unhealthy attitude may dislike or fear sex. They may be ashamed of their body.

Sexual practices or behavior form another part of sexuality. People differ in what gives them pleasure. For example, some people enjoy oral sex while others may dislike it.

Finally, sexuality is what arouses, or excites, a person's sexual desires. Likes and dislikes vary from person to person. Some people may be attracted to tall, skinny lovers. Others may like their partner to be plump and cuddly.

## Influences on Sexuality

Two main factors shape a person's sexuality. One factor is biological. The other is social. It can be difficult to separate these influences, which can be either positive or negative.

**According to one survey, teens today learn about sex from the following sources:**

Friends (45 percent)

Television (29 percent)

Parents (7 percent)

Sex-education classes (3 percent)

Biological factors refer to those parts of sexuality that people are born with. They include physical features such as the genitals, or sex organs. For males, this includes the penis and testicles. For females, it includes the vagina, uterus, and ovaries. But biological factors include more than sex organs. They involve the brain, nervous system, and hormones, too. The brain and nervous system perceive and react to sexual situations. Hormones are chemicals that cause physical changes in the body throughout a person's life.

Social factors are those parts of sexuality that people learn from life experiences. The minute a baby's sex is known, parents and other caregivers begin to shape the baby's sexuality. Later on, teachers and friends add their influence. Media, popular culture, religion, and laws influence a person's sexuality all through life. This book mainly focuses on the social influences that affect teen sexuality.

Your ideas about sexuality will change as you grow and develop. Since everyone's life experiences differ, no one's sexuality will be exactly the same as another's.

## Points to Consider

What are your ideas of masculine and feminine? Where do you think you got these ideas?

Ask a parent or other adult how ideas about gender role and identity have changed in the last 30 years. What are the differences?

How is your life different because you are male or female? What might your life be like if you were the opposite sex?

How does being sexy fit into sexuality?

## Chapter Overview

Everyone is sexual—even infants and senior citizens. Sexuality is a natural part of life.

Biological factors influence sexuality all through life.

Hormones are chemicals that affect growth and development. They also affect sexual feelings and desires.

The most dramatic biological, or physical, changes occur during puberty. These changes prepare males and females for reproduction.

Biological factors may influence differences in male and female sexual well-being.

# Chapter 2

## Biological Influences

Sexuality is a natural and healthy part of life. Everyone is sexual from birth to death. All human beings have sexual feelings, whether or not they act on them. It is possible to be sexual without ever having sex.

### The Sexual Journey

All through life, biological factors cause body changes, which affect sexuality. Knowing about these natural changes can help lessen your concerns and fears. Here's a brief overview of the different stages of sexuality. These stages are infancy, childhood, adolescence, young adulthood, midlife, and older adulthood.

### Infancy

The reflexes of infants respond to touch, which is an important part of sexuality. Babies have an inborn need to be held and stroked. Babies love to be hugged and cuddled by their parents and other caregivers. Babies explore their own body with their hands. This exploration includes touching their genitals.

**Did You Know?** Boys and girls split into homosocial groups around age 5 or 6. Homosocial means that boys play with boys and girls play with girls. They keep this gender division until puberty. Researchers have found the same pattern in India, Africa, Mexico, and the Philippines. They even have found the same pattern among animals. Biology as well as culture may affect the timing in changing friends.

### Childhood

Children enjoy touching themselves. Masturbation, or rubbing the genitals for pleasure, is a natural activity. During childhood, physical differences between boys and girls become more noticeable. Children naturally become curious about the body of others. "Playing doctor" or other sex play among friends is normal.

Changes in the body during this stage can affect a child's sense of being masculine or feminine. For example, a child may wonder, "Am I as tall as a boy or girl should be?"

### Adolescence

Adolescence is the stage beginning at puberty and ending at adulthood. Puberty can begin as early as age 9, but it also can start much later. During puberty, hormones cause physical changes in the body. These changes prepare males and females for reproduction.

The female hormones estrogen and progesterone cause a teen girl's breasts to develop. Her uterus and vagina grow. The ovaries start to release eggs. If a sperm, or male sex cell, doesn't fertilize an egg, the lining of the uterus is shed. This shedding occurs about once a month and is the girl's menstrual period. Girls experience other physical changes during puberty. These include growing taller, getting bigger hips, and developing thicker, darker hair under the arms and on the legs.

The male hormone testosterone causes a teen boy's penis and testicles to get bigger. The testicles start to make millions of sperm. The boy can now ejaculate, or release semen, the fluid that contains sperm. This may occur during sleep. Ejaculating at this time is sometimes called having a wet dream. Ejaculation also may occur during masturbation or sexual activity with a partner.

Teen boys have many spontaneous, or unplanned, erections because of the high level of testosterone in their body. During an erection, the penis gets hard and stands away from the body. Other physical changes boys experience include growing taller and stronger and developing facial hair and a deeper voice.

The physical changes of puberty can cause teens emotional distress. Girls may worry about the size of their breasts or think they're getting fat. Boys may worry about the size of their penis. Both girls and boys may be concerned about masturbation and sexual dreams and thoughts. They wonder if anyone will find them sexually attractive. Most teens overcome these anxieties, but sometimes adolescent experiences can have a lasting effect on sexuality.

Maddie was an "early bloomer." Her **Maddie, Age 18** breasts started to develop when she was 10 years old. She was the only girl in her fifth-grade class to wear a bra. The boys often stared at her. They teased her and called her names. Maddie tried to hide her breasts by wearing oversized shirts. Maddie still remembers how embarrassed she felt. Even now, she feels a little self-conscious about her body at times.

**Into the Future**

Scientists are studying the possibility that smell, not looks or personality, attracts human beings to each other. According to this theory, pheromones relay information about a person's emotional state, physical health, and sexual availability. Pheromones are scents that humans may sense but not smell.

Hormones also create strong sexual feelings and desires and can cause teens to be moody. Adolescents may begin to find themselves attracted to a sexual partner.

### Young Adulthood

During young adulthood, physical changes begin to level off, and hormones become more balanced. A woman's menstrual cycle usually becomes more regular. A man tends to have fewer spontaneous erections and wet dreams. Both men and women may feel an urge to settle down and enjoy a close sexual relationship.

Hormonal changes during pregnancy can affect a woman's sexuality. Her desire for intercourse may increase or decrease. Pregnancy affects sexual practices with her partner, such as intercourse positions. Many women breastfeed their infant. Breastfeeding causes the uterus to contract. When the uterus does this and becomes smaller, it's often sexually pleasurable for the woman.

### Midlife

Midlife generally extends from age 40 to age 55. During this time, most women go through menopause. This is when their menstrual cycles stop, and they no longer can have children. Their ovaries produce less estrogen, which can affect sexual desire. Many women enjoy intercourse more after menopause because they no longer worry about getting pregnant.

Men during this time experience a decrease in testosterone, which can slow down sexual response. It may take longer to develop an erection. The penis and testicles become smaller.

Women and men in midlife once again may become anxious about body changes. They may wonder if they still are attractive to a sexual partner. They may worry about being able to perform sexually.

**Older Adulthood**

Older adults also have sexual needs, even if their reproductive years are over. Changes in their body may make sexual intercourse more difficult. For example, the vagina may shrink in size and width, and the walls may become thinner. Poor circulation, or blood flow, may make having an erection more difficult. Many older adults satisfy their need for physical closeness in ways other than intercourse. Caressing, embracing, and kissing may become more important.

## Male and Female Differences in Sexuality

Males and females tend to differ in what they need for sexual well-being. This especially is true for younger men and women. Women tend to place more importance on intimacy, or closeness, than on sexual intercourse. They want long-lasting, loving relationships, and they want intercourse to be special. Men tend to place more importance on sexual performance. They may be less willing than women to commit to a relationship. Partners need to communicate their needs in order to have a satisfying relationship.

"I let Sam talk me into having sex. I really didn't want to do it, but I thought having sex would draw us closer together. It hasn't made any difference, though. All Sam wants now is sex."

**Jody, Age 16**

"So Jody and I had sex. What's the big deal? Now she acts like she owns me. She wants to hold hands in public and act like we're a couple. I'm just not ready for all that mushy stuff."

**Sam, Age 17**

Scientists believe that biological factors may explain male and female differences in sexual well-being. Here's one theory. Beginning in prehistoric times, males and females have played different roles in the survival of the human race. Some scientists believe that females have a nesting instinct. They settle down to nurse and shelter their young. These scientists believe that males, on the other hand, have an instinct to roam and scatter their sperm with females. The more sperm they release, the greater the chances of making a female pregnant and continuing the race.

Females tend to be better with words than males. Males tend to have a better sense of space and distance. Differences in brain size, structure, and function may be responsible for these and other gender differences. The female brain is smaller than the male brain but more densely packed with neurons, or brain cells. Females and males use their brain in different ways.

Here's another theory. Males produce millions of sperm. Because of this, some researchers believe that a single act of intercourse doesn't seem that important to men. In comparison, females produce only one egg per month. These researchers believe that because of this, females want to find a male whose genes will produce the best baby. Further research should result in more information on biological differences in male and female sexuality.

## Points to Consider

Why is it important for females to know about male biological changes? Why is it important for males to know about female changes?

Why is going through puberty difficult for many teens?

What are some differences in the way males and females behave? Do you think males and females are born this way, or are they taught to be different?

Do you think females want to make love while males want to have sex? Explain.

## Chapter Overview

Parents and other caregivers help children acquire gender identity and gender role. These adults usually teach qualities and behaviors that fit society's definitions of masculine and feminine.

Traditional ideas about gender identity and gender role are changing. Less emphasis is placed on what is masculine and what is feminine.

Parents who provide loving, dependable care help their children develop trust. Being able to trust another person is important for a mature sexual relationship.

Parents say and do many things that influence a child's ideas and feelings about sex. Attitudes learned in childhood can affect adult sexuality.

Parents can have a positive influence on teen sexual behavior by answering questions about sex and helping teens establish values.

# Chapter 3

## Family Influences

Parents and other caregivers play a major part in shaping a child's sexuality. They help to establish the child's gender identity and gender role. They also teach attitudes about sex and sexual behavior. These attitudes may affect the child's intimate relationships later in life.

### Gender Identity

Parents begin the process of gender identity by giving their newborn a "girl's" name or a "boy's" name. They may dress a little girl in fancy pink dresses and put ribbons in her hair. They may dress a little boy in blue pants and shirts. Parents also may use these colors to decorate the child's room in either a masculine or feminine style.

Parents usually raise their children to fit society's ideas of masculine or feminine. For example, males in the United States and Canada generally are expected to hold back their emotions. As a result, parents may discourage boys from crying when they are hurt or sad. It's generally more acceptable for girls to show their feelings.

### Gender Role

Society expects males and females to perform different functions. One way parents teach gender role is by the toys that they give their children. They may give girls dolls, a play stove, sink, and dishes. These toys suggest that little girls are expected to become mothers and homemakers. Parents may give boys trucks, toy guns, and baseball bats to play with. These toys may help boys see themselves in a variety of roles.

Parents also teach gender role through household tasks. Girls often are expected to wash dishes, dust, vacuum, and do other housework. Boys often are expected to help with yard work and household repairs. Girls may learn to cook, sew, and do laundry. Boys may learn to oil squeaky doors, change tires, and fix leaky faucets.

## Changing Expectations

Ideas about gender identity and gender role are changing. Many of today's parents avoid following traditional ideas of masculine and feminine. For example, they may decide not to use pink for girls and blue for boys. Instead, they may decorate their child's room in gender-neutral colors such as yellow or green. They may let boys play with dolls and girls play with trucks and cars. These parents believe that traditional ideas deny opportunities to both boys and girls. They want their children to have a variety of experiences and to be able to choose what feels right for them.

"My dad wants me to be a strong and independent woman. He says there won't always be a man around to help me. He gave me a toolbox for my birthday and showed me how to use all the tools. Now I can pound a nail straight, unclog a drain, tighten loose screws, and make many other repairs. I feel proud of myself."

**Luz, Age 17**

"My mom says she won't always be around to clean up after me. She got me into the habit of hanging up my clothes and picking up after myself. She's even made sure I know how to sew on a button and cook a few things. I know I'll be able to survive when I get my own place someday."

**Dayo, Age 16**

### Building Trust and Self-Esteem

Trust is an important part of a healthy sexual relationship. Couples must be able to trust each other before they can share physical and emotional intimacy. People begin to learn trust as infants and children. Children whose parents love them and take care of their needs develop trust. Later on, they're able to transfer this feeling to other relationships. Children whose parents neglect them or abuse them may fear intimate relationships as adults.

Self-esteem is another important part of healthy sexuality. People who feel good about themselves are likely to be open and caring to others. Parents and other caregivers can help children develop self-esteem. These adults can praise children, point out their good qualities, and help them develop skills and interests.

### Attitudes Toward Sexuality

Parents have many opportunities to influence their children's attitude toward sexuality. Their words and behavior can contribute to either healthy or unhealthy sexual attitudes. Ideas learned as a child may stay with a person for the rest of his or her life. The following chart shows ways that parents help to develop sexual attitudes.

Even if parents don't talk about sex, they still send messages to their children. Silent messages may make children think that sex is unimportant, uncomfortable, or dangerous.

Did You Know?

## Ways Parents Help to Develop Healthy Sexuality

Hold and touch child lovingly

Tell child that masturbation is normal but that it should be done in private

Use correct terms for penis, vagina, and other sex organs

Handle nudity in the family in a matter-of-fact way

Openly show affection for each other

Share sexual values with their child, such as respect for the opposite sex

Tell child about sex in terms appropriate to his or her level of understanding

Prepare child well in advance about menstruation, erections, and other body changes

## Ways Parents Help to Develop Unhealthy Sexuality

Seldom hug or kiss child

Punish or scold child for masturbating

Use street words such as "peepee" and "boobies" for body parts

Become upset or embarrassed if child sees them naked

Seldom show affection for each other

Never talk about sex

Do not prepare child for the natural changes in his or her body

Many teens today grow up in families where parents work long hours away from home. Teens have more unsupervised time at home to experiment with sex. As one teen said, "My mom never gets home until 6:30. My girlfriend and I can use my bed or the couch and no one bothers us."

## Teens and Family Influences

Parents can have a big influence on the sexual behavior of their teen children. Teens have many questions about dating, romantic relationships, sex, and birth control. They often want help setting limits on sexual activity and saying no to pressure to have sex. Most teens would like to be able to talk with their parents about these matters.

### Talking With Parents About Sex

Talking with your parents about sex can be hard. Both teens and parents may feel uncomfortable, especially if the family has not talked openly about sex in the past. Parents may feel they don't know enough facts, or they may be uncertain how they feel about teens having sex. Today, many parents work long hours outside the home and have little time for talks with their children. Despite these difficulties, it's important for you to talk with a parent or caretaker. Here are some pointers.

Influences on Sexuality

Ask for some quiet time for a talk. This should be a time when there will be few distractions.

Use a conversation starter such as a magazine article or TV show about teen sex.

Say something like, "I know we've never talked about this, but I'd like to know . . ." or "This is hard for me to ask you, but . . ."

Remember that your parents may be uncomfortable if their parents never talked with them about sex.

Assure parents that wanting information about sex doesn't mean you're planning to go right out and try it. Teens need the facts so they can make responsible decisions.

Tell your parents how much it means to you to be able to talk with them instead of someone else.

**The National Longitudinal Study of Adolescent Health is the biggest survey of U.S. teens ever conducted. According to this study, teens believe that parents are an important part of their life. Parents can help their teens avoid risky sexual behavior by doing the following:**

Sending clear messages about what they want their teens to do and not do

Spending time with them

Talking with them

Being available to them

Setting high standards

"My parents told me about sex when I was just a kid. When I had my first wet dream, I wasn't scared. I knew what was happening to me. My parents talk with me about right and wrong sexual behavior. For instance, they said it was wrong for guys to demand sex from girls. They've taught me to respect girls."

Brad, Age 14

## Points to Consider

What are advantages and disadvantages of gender identities and roles?

Why do you think ideas about gender roles are changing?

How did your parents or caregivers shape your gender identity and gender role? Is there anything you wish were different? Explain.

How might growing up in a single-parent home influence a child's sexuality?

How would you describe your family's attitude toward sexuality? Is there an adult you can talk with about sex?

## Chapter Overview

Children and teens learn about sexuality from people their own age. Peer influences are strongest during the teen years.

Peers can influence how teens behave as males or females. They provide information about sex. Peers sometimes put pressure on each other to have sexual intercourse.

Children and teens may learn about sexuality in sex-education classes at school. They also may learn about sexuality indirectly through the attitudes, values, and behaviors of their teachers.

Some people believe that traditional education favors the development of boys over girls. Gender equity attempts to make opportunities equal for boys and girls.

## Chapter 4

# Peer and School Influences

Children and teens learn about sexuality from their peers, or people their own age. They also learn about sexuality from experiences in school.

## Peer Influences

Peer influences on sexuality begin in childhood. Children learn what boys do and what girls do through their play activities. Children put pressure on each other to act and dress in certain ways. They may tease or ridicule a child who doesn't fit their idea of masculine or feminine.

Peer influences become strongest during the teen years. Teens look to their peer group for support as they begin the process of separating from their family. Friends and classmates influence teen sexuality in several ways.

### Gender Identity and Roles

Teens usually have sharply defined gender roles and rules about sexual behavior. Boys often are expected to become sexually aggressive or to act manly. They may be pushed into having sexual intercourse because they believe that's what boys do. Girls may spend their time making themselves as attractive as possible to boys. They may put less effort into their schoolwork because they believe boys dislike girls who are smart and ambitious. Teens must decide for themselves if they want to take on such roles.

### Sexual Attitudes

Teens get a great deal of information about sex from their friends. Talking with friends about sex can be fun, but friends often have wrong information. This incorrect information sometimes can make sex seem like something dirty.

Girls Incorporated is an organization that teaches girls about their sexuality. The program begins with girls as young as 9 years old and follows them through high school. Educational and career planning is a major focus of the program, too. The organization has shown that girls who are excited about their future are likely to avoid an unplanned teen pregnancy.

**Pressure to Have Sex**

Peers can have a lot of influence on a teen's decisions regarding sexual activity. Friends and boyfriends or girlfriends may try to pressure other teens into having sex. They may say things like "Everyone's doing it" or "You need to prove you're a man (or a woman)." Many teens have sex because they fear being rejected by peers if they don't follow along.

Teens who are pushed into having sex usually are not ready for the experience. They risk an unplanned pregnancy, an STD, or emotional hurt. Having sex too early can affect a person's sexual attitudes and behavior for a long time.

**Marisa, Age 17**

Marisa had sex for the first time when she was 15. She gave in to pressure from her boyfriend, James. Afterward, Marisa felt mad that she had let it happen. She also was sad because she knew her mother wouldn't approve. Marisa stopped dating James and hasn't had sex since. "When I have sex again, it will be with someone I really care about," she says. "I don't want to feel that out of control ever again."

Teens can learn to stand up against peer pressure to have sex. Here are just a few ideas:

**Set limits on your sexual activity.** Decide ahead of time what you will and will not do.

**Be up front with your friends and boyfriend or girlfriend about your decision not to have sex.** If they know your position, they may be less likely to pressure you.

**Hang around with friends who believe as you do.** You can enjoy nonsexual activities together.

**Stay away from risky situations.** Parties with alcohol or other drugs can be risky. Being home alone with a boyfriend or girlfriend can sometimes lead to unsafe behavior.

**Learn to be assertive.** Assertive is different from aggressive. Aggressiveness is being pushy. Assertiveness is stating firmly and clearly what you believe.

## School Influences

Children and teens may learn about sexuality through formal, or planned, sex-education instruction. However, they are more likely to learn about sexuality indirectly from teachers, textbooks, and school activities.

**Sex Education**

Sex education in U.S. public schools is controversial. Some people want sex education to be taught only in the home. They believe parents have the right to control what to teach their children about sex and sexual values and morals. Other people want schools to teach sex education. They may believe many parents are unwilling or unable to do the job.

At the present time, local school districts decide whether to teach sex education and the topics to be covered. No nationwide standard exists. Some districts provide no sex education at all. Other districts teach abstinence-only sex education. Abstinence means postponing, or delaying, sexual relations. Still other districts present the facts about pregnancy, STDs, and birth control. Some schools may go beyond the facts and teach sexual values and morals. However, this, too, is controversial. Not everyone agrees on what is right and wrong sexual behavior.

**Indirect Lessons on Sexuality**

Several studies have shown that teachers, educational materials, and school activities influence students' gender identity and role. The studies suggest one thing in particular about traditional education in the United States. It has caused girls to see themselves as less capable or less important than boys.

**Teachers.** Teachers' attitudes, values, and behaviors can influence how students see themselves. Both male and female teachers have different expectations of boys and girls. According to research, many teachers tend to do the following:

Give girls less attention than boys

Encourage more boys than girls to think independently

Scold girls but not boys for speaking out of turn

Evaluate girls' work on its appearance (for example, neatness of handwriting) while they evaluate boys' work on its content

Encourage boys to prepare for careers in math and science

**Educational materials.** Textbooks, films, and other educational materials tend to emphasize male achievements throughout history. References to the achievements of women are limited.

**Classes.** In the past, girls took home economics (cooking and sewing classes). Boys took industrial arts (classes in woodworking, electricity, and metalwork). These class assignments reinforced, or strengthened, traditional gender-role stereotypes. In most schools today, both girls and boys must take beginning courses in home economics and industrial arts. However, it's still more common for girls to take advanced home economics and boys to take advanced industrial arts.

### Gender Equity

During the last 20 years, a movement called gender equity has attempted to ensure equal opportunities for boys and girls. The word *equity* means "equal." The gender-equity movement has achieved many things. One of the most significant achievements has been more opportunities for girls to participate in competitive athletics.

Some people criticize the gender-equity movement. They believe it hasn't accomplished equality for the sexes. Girls, they say, have benefited more than boys. For example, it's now common to urge girls to become doctors or scientists. However, boys generally are not encouraged to pursue traditional female activities such as dance or poetry writing. Critics of the gender-equity movement point to ways schools are unfair to boys. They believe that instead of focusing on gender, schools should treat boys and girls as individuals.

## Points to Consider

What are the social roles for boys and girls in your school? Do boys and girls respect each other?

Is peer pressure to have sex a problem in your school? Explain.

Does your school provide equal opportunities for boys and girls in academics, sports, and other areas? Explain.

Do you think sex education should be taught in school? Why or why not?

## Chapter Overview

The media and popular culture have a strong influence on teens' sexual values, attitudes, and behavior.

Portrayals of sex in the media may give teens the idea that casual sex is common, that people don't talk about sex before it happens, and that unprotected sex has no risks.

Movies and TV shows tend to use stereotypes for male, female, gay, and lesbian characters.

Teens can create a demand for portrayals of healthy sexuality in the media.

Teens shouldn't let images of the ideal body in ads and in TV shows and movies damage their self-confidence.

# Chapter 5

## Influences From the Media and Popular Culture

The media includes television, movies, newspapers, magazines, books, advertising, and, most recently, the Internet. Popular culture refers to things people in a community share, such as language, fashions, and music. The media and popular culture often encourage unhealthy sexual attitudes and behaviors among teens.

### Surrounded by Sex

Teens today live in a world in which sex is everywhere. It appears on billboards, in the lyrics to popular songs, and in newspaper headlines. Nowhere is sex more common than on television. According to one estimate, TV exposes the average teen to 14,000 sexual messages each year.

On MTV, 75 percent of videos that tell a story use sexual images. Over half involve violence, and 80 percent combine sex and violence.

### Sex in the Media

The sexual content of TV shows, movies, music videos, and other media may be direct or indirect. There may be scenes of couples kissing passionately, taking off each other's clothes, and preparing for intercourse. This is direct, in-your-face sex. Indirect content includes comedians making jokes about sex or talk-show hosts discussing the sex lives of their guests.

Sexual scenes in the media usually feature young and attractive people. They may have just met. These people rarely discuss the possibility of an unplanned pregnancy or an STD.

### Effects of Sex in the Media

The media has a powerful influence on teens' sexual values, attitudes, and beliefs. Constant exposure to sexual images can make teens indifferent to sex. They may view sex as something couples automatically do in a relationship. Teens may lose appreciation for love. Sex even may seem boring.

> "Sex is everywhere, even in my skateboarding magazine. It's become so normal it doesn't even affect you. There's sex in comic books. On talk shows, people constantly talk about such things as sleeping with their best friend's wife. There's just too much talk about sex."
>
> **Freddie, Age 13**

Sex in the media can give teens the idea that they don't need to protect themselves from pregnancy and disease. They see their favorite actors and actresses having sex and believe that having sex will make them seem mature. They may be pushed into having sex before they're ready.

Teens may learn a great deal about the physical side of sexual intercourse from the media. However, TV shows and movies usually don't show how sex affects people emotionally and how it affects relationships. The importance of respect and communication in a relationship isn't emphasized.

## Sexual Stereotypes in the Media

Teens look to the media to tell them how to act as males or females. The media tends to reinforce stereotypes of masculine and feminine behavior. According to many TV shows and movies, women and girls are concerned with romance and dating while men are concerned with work. Teen magazines geared toward teen girls focus on beauty, dating, and friendships.

In recent years, the media has improved its portrayal, or representation, of women. They are shown more often as independent, intelligent people. They often are single and working. Teen magazines devote more space to teen issues such as choosing a career or the effects of drugs and smoking.

The media also tends to reinforce stereotypes of gays and lesbians. Gays and lesbians do have more TV and movie roles than in the past. However, they often are cast as comic sidekicks to main characters. The media tends to focus on sexual orientation rather than show gays and lesbians as individuals.

### Teens and the Media

The media itself is neither good nor bad. It's how people use it that counts. The media can help promote healthy sexual attitudes and behaviors. The list of suggestions on the next page from Advocates for Youth shows how the media can be more responsible. You can do your part by becoming a critical consumer of the media. This could include the following:

Watching TV programs and movies that portray healthy sexuality

Writing or e-mailing TV networks and asking them to include more realistic story lines about sex

Refusing to buy videos and other products with heavy sexual content

Realizing that most people do not act like soap-opera characters in real life

## Guide to Responsible Sexual Content in Television, Films, and Music

Show that young, unmarried, and beautiful people are not the only ones in sexual relationships.

Show that affection and touching do not always end in sex.

Show couples who have love and respect for each other in sexual relationships.

Show or discuss the consequences of unprotected sex.

Do not use a miscarriage as a dramatic way to conveniently resolve an unplanned pregnancy. A miscarriage is a pregnancy that ends too early.

Show that contraceptive use is a normal part of a sexual relationship.

Avoid associating violence with sex or love.

Depict, or show, rape only as a crime of violence, not as one of passion.

Recognize and respect the ability to say no.

Fifty percent of ads in leading teen magazines use beauty to sell their products.

### The Ideal Body

Body image is another area in which the media and popular culture have a major impact on teens, especially teen girls. Advertisements, TV shows, and movies feature beautiful, young women and handsome, young men. The women are ultra thin, and the men are muscular and well-toned. They all have high cheekbones, straight noses, large eyes, and white teeth.

The ideal body portrayed in the media is impossible for most people to achieve. Nevertheless, many teens see this image and become unhappy with their own body. They may go to extreme lengths to look more like their favorite models, singers, and TV stars. Some teens try things such as excessive dieting or even plastic surgery. They may let negative feelings about their body affect their self-esteem. If you are letting the media influence your body image, here are some things to remember:

**Advertisers want you to feel bad about yourself.** They want you to worry about body odor, oily hair, pimples, and extra pounds. If you worry about these things, you are more likely to buy their products.

**Models and TV and movie stars have makeup artists and hair stylists to make them look good.** Photographers use special lenses and airbrush photos to hide blemishes, wrinkles, and other flaws celebrities have.

**Everyone can find something they like about their body.**
Perhaps you have great hair, a winning smile, or beautiful
eyes. Be glad about your good points. Think, too, of all the
amazing things your body does. You may have a new
appreciation of yourself.

**Sex appeal is more than good looks.** Talk with couples who
are in love. Ask what drew them to each other. More than
likely it was not an ideal body.

## Points to Consider

Watch prime-time, or evening, TV for a week. Keep a record
of the number of sexual situations or references you see or
hear. What effect do these messages have on your feelings
and attitudes toward sex?

How do today's fashions influence sexuality?

How could you help a friend have a positive body image?

Do you think public-service announcements on TV and on
the radio promote healthy sexuality? Give an example.

## Chapter Overview

Most religions have teachings about sex and sexuality. These teachings can influence a person's sexual attitudes and behavior.

Religious teachings can contribute to a positive or negative view of sexuality.

Every community has laws regarding sexual behavior. These laws are meant to reflect what people in the community believe is acceptable and unacceptable sexual behavior.

Sexual laws attempt to regulate, or control, sexual behavior. Some of these laws are controversial. Laws can protect people from sexual abuse and provide a standard of decency in a community.

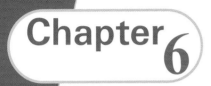

# Chapter 6

## Religious and Legal Influences

### Religious Influences

Christianity, Judaism, Islam, and other religions have teachings and values about sex and sexuality. These teachings relate to some of the following subjects:

How to regard the body

Masturbation

The purpose of sex

Sex before marriage

Sexual orientation

Duties of husband and wife

Faithfulness to marriage partner

Religious teachings can contribute to healthy sexuality. For example, many religions teach that the body is good and that people should love and respect each other. These are positive aspects of sexuality.

Rocky belongs to a church that serves **Rocky, Age 19** gays and lesbians. He likes being able to worship with people who love and accept him. He also can meet new friends and participate in social activities at his church.

Religious teachings also can contribute to unhealthy sexual attitudes. For example, some people learn from their religion that the body is bad and that sex is sinful. As a result, they may avoid sexual relationships or they may be unable to get pleasure from sexual intercourse.

Influences on Sexuality

Sex laws reflect the beliefs of a group of people. The laws can vary greatly from one society to another. Among the Inuit people in the Arctic, it is acceptable for husbands to share their wife with male guests. In Afghanistan, on the other hand, husbands and wives may be stoned to death for having sex outside marriage. In some societies, teen boys and girls are kept apart until marriage. In other societies, children are encouraged to have sexual intercourse before puberty.

Teens must decide for themselves the importance of religious teachings in their life. Religious values can help teens make decisions about their sexual behavior. For example, many religions teach that sex outside marriage is wrong. Some teens base their decision to be abstinent on this teaching.

Rachel has chosen to follow the laws and customs of Orthodox Judaism. She

**Rachel, Age 18**

wears long skirts and sleeves that cover her elbows for the sake of modesty. She follows a custom for unmarried women, which says that she cannot touch men. Rachel cherishes these laws. She wants to remain abstinent until marriage. Rachel believes the laws help her be pure in body and spirit.

## Legal Influences

Lawmakers pass laws that regulate, or control, sexual behavior. People learn from these laws what they should or should not do sexually. There are two main groups of sex laws. One group protects people against sexual abuse. The other group promotes moral, or decent, behavior.

### Laws That Protect Against Sexual Abuse

Some types of sexual behavior clearly are wrong because they hurt people. These behaviors include the following:

Pedophilia (sexual contact between adults and children)

Incest (sexual activity between members of the same family)

Rape (forced sexual intercourse)

Sexual harassment (unwanted sexual attention)

Victims of these crimes may suffer serious, lifelong problems such as depression or an eating disorder. They may have feelings of deep shame and guilt. Sex-crime victims themselves may go on to hurt others. For example, an adult who has sexual contact with children may have been sexually abused as a child. Teens who have been sexually abused must tell a trusted adult so they can get the help they need.

### Laws That Promote Moral Behavior

Some sex laws promote moral behavior. These laws usually reflect the religious or political views of certain groups of people. For example, there are laws against same-sex marriages and laws against oral and anal intercourse. These laws reflect religious teachings that sexual intercourse should only be for reproduction.

Some laws apply to the sexual behavior of teens. These include the following:

**Age of Consent Laws:** The age at which a teen is considered old enough to agree to have sex

**Reproductive Rights Laws:** Laws guaranteeing teens confidential, or private, access to birth control and testing and treatment of STDs

**Teen Pregnancy and Welfare Laws:** Laws requiring pregnant teens to live with a parent or finish high school in order to receive welfare. Such laws are designed to discourage teens from becoming pregnant.

Laws about moral behavior tend to be controversial. Not everyone agrees that the behaviors they regulate are wrong. Laws against prostitution (buying and selling sexual acts) and pornography (sexual images considered obscene, or indecent) belong to this group.

## Points to Consider

Have any religious teachings influenced your sexuality? Explain.

What is the age of consent where you live? What other laws regulate teen sexual behavior? From these laws, what can you tell about your community's beliefs regarding teen sexuality?

Where could a teen who has been sexually abused go for help in your community?

## Chapter Overview

Knowing about the influences on sexuality can help teens in many ways.

Influences on sexuality affect the choices teens make regarding sexual behavior and attitudes.

Teens often face situations and problems related to sexuality.

Communication helps people to understand the influences on each other's sexuality.

# Chapter 7

## How Understanding Influences Can Help

Knowing about influences on sexuality is important for everyone. It's especially important for teens because they are at a critical stage in their sexual development. Knowing about influences on sexuality can help you do the following:

Understand your sexual feelings and desires

Be comfortable with your body image, gender identity, and sexual orientation

Decide on your gender role

Learn to respect your sexuality and the sexuality of others

Make healthy choices regarding your sexual behavior

Sexual attitudes have changed greatly during the last 50 years. During the 1950s, sex outside marriage was regarded as sinful. Girls who were pregnant and unwed were scorned. Beginning in the 1960s, the widespread use of the birth control pill led to a sexual revolution. Without the fear of pregnancy, people had sex more freely and with more partners. Then, in the 1990s, the fear of AIDS caused many people to limit their sexual activity once again.

### Making Healthy Choices

Teens must make many choices regarding sexuality. The different influences on sexuality can make choosing the best alternative difficult. Various influences may give teens mixed messages. For example, parents and religious leaders may urge teens not to have sex. Peers and the media may make sex seem like the most important thing in the world. Being aware of influences on sexuality, however, is a start toward making healthy choices.

### Situations and Problems Regarding Sexuality

Teens may encounter many different situations or problems regarding sexuality. Some situations may be more serious than others. The questions in the following chart can help you identify issues related to your sexuality. Serious problems such as sexual abuse or fear of intimacy may require the help of a trained therapist. This person can talk with you and help you solve specific problems.

## How Do You Feel About Your Sexuality?

**Answer yes or no to each of the following statements.**

1. I like my body..................................... Yes   No

2. I like my gender.................................. Yes   No

3. I feel comfortable with my gender role.......... Yes   No

4. I feel comfortable with my sexual orientation.... Yes   No

5. I like and respect peers of the opposite sex....... Yes   No

6. I know the facts about pregnancy and STDs...... Yes   No

7. I feel comfortable talking with my parents
   about sex......................................... Yes   No

8. I have set limits on my sexual activity........... Yes   No

9. I have a healthy attitude toward sexual
   intercourse...................................... Yes   No

10. I know what is right and wrong
    sexual behavior.................................. Yes   No

If you answered yes to all these statements, you probably have
a healthy sexuality. If you answered no to any statement, you
may want to do some problem solving.

**Did You Know?**

Certain injuries, diseases, and other health conditions can affect a person's sexuality. People with arthritis may find it difficult to have intercourse. People with depression may lose interest in sexual activity. People with cancer may feel unattractive because of hair loss, tiredness, and sickness.

Teens facing a situation or problem related to sexuality should get the facts. The correct information provides understanding. Do some reading or talk with a person who knows the facts.

Remember that influences can be positive or negative. If you're not sure which is which, think about motives. Is someone trying to sell you something? Is someone trying to get you in trouble? Is someone using you to satisfy his or her own needs? Or, is someone looking out for your best interests? A positive influence on sexuality may be able to guide you in making a healthy decision.

## Communication

Now that you're aware of the influences on your sexuality, talk with others, especially possible partners, about your sexuality. This helps other people know how to relate to you. Try to find a quiet time and place to talk. Remember that other people have different influences. Respect their sexuality and encourage others to do the same.

## Points to Consider

Think of some people who have different ideas about sexuality than you do. What do you think were their influences?

Here are examples of situations in which teens must make choices about sexuality. What aspect of sexuality does each involve? What influences might enter into their decision making?

> Situation 1. Sasha is an outstanding basketball player. Although her school has a girls' basketball team, Sasha wants to play on the boys' team. She doesn't think the girls' team is challenging enough for her.

> Situation 2. Chad worries that he has too many erections. He spends a lot of time thinking and dreaming about sex. "Why can't I concentrate on anything else?" he wonders.

> Situation 3. Jack's teacher asked him to work with Art on a science project. Jack feels uncomfortable because Art is gay.

Can you think of influences on sexuality other than those described in this book? What are they?

# Glossary

**attitude** (AT-i-tood)—beliefs and feelings about someone or something

**feminine** (FEM-uh-nuhn)—relating to women

**gender** (JEN-dur)—male or female

**heterosexual** (het-er-oh-SEK-shoo-wuhl)—relating to the attraction to people of the opposite gender

**homosexual** (hoh-moh-SEK-shoo-wuhl)—relating to the attraction to people of the same gender

**hormone** (HOR-mohn)—a chemical that controls sexual development and body functions

**influence** (IN-floo-uhnss)—to have an effect on someone or something

**intimacy** (IN-tuh-muh-see)—closeness

**masculine** (MASS-kyuh-lin)—relating to men

**puberty** (PYOO-bur-tee)—the time when a person's body changes from a child's to an adult's

**sexual intercouse** (SEK-shoo-wuhl IN-tur-korss)—penetration of the penis into the vagina, anus, or mouth

**sexual orientation** (SEK-shoo-wuhl or-ee-uhn-TAY-shuhn)—sexual attraction, behavior, or desire for others based on gender

**stereotype** (STER-ee-oh-tipe)—an overly simple picture or opinion of a person, group, or thing

**traditional** (truh-DISH-uh-nuhl)—relating to a custom, idea, or belief that is handed down from one generation to the next

**value** (val-YOO)—a person's belief or idea about what is important in life

## For More Information

Bell, Ruth. *Changing Bodies, Changing Lives: A Book for Teens on Sex and Relationships.* 3d ed. New York: Times Books, 1998.

Endersbe, Julie K. *Healthy Sexuality: What Is It?* Mankato, MN: Capstone, 2000.

Gurian, Michael. *Understanding Guys: A Guide for Teenage Girls.* New York: Price Stern Sloan, 1999.

Rosenberg, Ellen. *Growing Up Feeling Good.* New York: Puffin Books, 1995.

# Useful Addresses and Internet Sites

Kaiser Family Foundation
2400 Sand Hill Road
Menlo Park, CA 94025
www.kff.org

Planned Parenthood Federation of America
810 Seventh Avenue
New York, NY 10019
1-800-669-0156
www.plannedparenthood.org

Planned Parenthood Federation of Canada
1 Nicholas Street, Suite 430
Ottawa, ON K1N 7B7
CANADA
www.ppfc.ca

Sexuality Information and Education Council
of the United States (SIECUS)
130 West 42nd Street, Suite 350
New York, NY 10036-7802
www.siecus.org

Kids Help Phone in Canada
kidshelp.sympatico.ca
Contains information, tips, and links that teens
can use when facing life's challenges

Sex, Etc.
www.sxetc.org
Provides articles on sexuality written by teens
for teens

Sexuality Education Resource Centre
Manitoba
www.serc.mb.ca/faqs.htm
Provides answers to some frequently asked
questions, as well as links to other helpful sites

teenwire
www.teenwire.com
Covers a variety of topics related to sexuality
and relationships

National Youth Crisis Hot Line
1-800-448-4663

# Index

abstinence, 51
adolescence, 15, 16–18
Advocates for Youth, 44–45
Age of Consent Laws, 53
AIDS, 56
assertiveness, 36
attitudes, 11, 35, 38, 57
    changing, 56
    family influences on, 23, 26, 56
    media influences on, 41–43, 44, 56
    peer influences on, 34
    religious influences on, 49–51, 56
    teachers' influences on, 38

behaviors, 11, 35
    family influences on, 26, 56
    legal influences on, 51–53
    media influences on, 41–43, 44, 56
    moral, 51, 52–53
    peer influences on, 33–36, 56
    religious influences on, 51
    teachers' influences on, 36, 38
beliefs, 42, 51
bisexuality, 10
body image, 5, 6, 46–47, 55, 57
brain, 12, 21
breastfeeding, 18
breasts, 16, 17

childhood, 10, 15, 16, 23, 26, 33
choices, 55, 56
classes, 38
communication, 19, 43, 58

dreams, 17

educational materials, 38
eggs, 16, 21
ejaculation, 17
emotions, 5, 17–18, 24, 35, 43
erections, 17, 18, 19, 27

estrogen, 16, 18
expectations, 8, 9, 25

femininity, 7, 16, 23–25, 33, 43
friends, 12, 34, 36

gays, 10, 11, 44, 50
gender
    differences, 19–21
    equity, 39
    identity, 5, 7, 8, 23–24, 25, 34, 37, 55, 57
    roles, 5, 8–9, 23, 24, 25, 34, 37, 38, 55, 57
genetics, 10
Girls Incorporated, 35

health, 26, 27, 55, 56, 57, 58
heterosexuality, 10
homosexuality, 10, 11
homosocial groups, 16
hormones, 7, 12, 16–18

incest, 52
infancy, 15, 26
information, 34, 58
instincts, 20
intercourse, 5, 28
    and gender roles, 9, 21, 34
    in the media, 43
    in older adulthood, 19
    and pregnancy, 18
    religious influences on, 50, 51, 52
    risks of, 11
intimacy, 19, 26, 56

lesbians, 10, 11, 44, 50
likes and dislikes, 5, 11
love, 19, 42, 45, 47

magazines, 29, 43, 46

06/01

DATE DUE

| | | | |
|---|---|---|---|
| | | | |
| | | | |
| | | | |
| | | | |
| | | | |
| | | | |
| | | | |
| | | | |
| | | | |
| | | | |
| | | | |
| | | | |
| | | | |
| | | | |
| | | | |
| | | | |
| | | | |
| GAYLORD | | | PRINTED IN U.S.A |